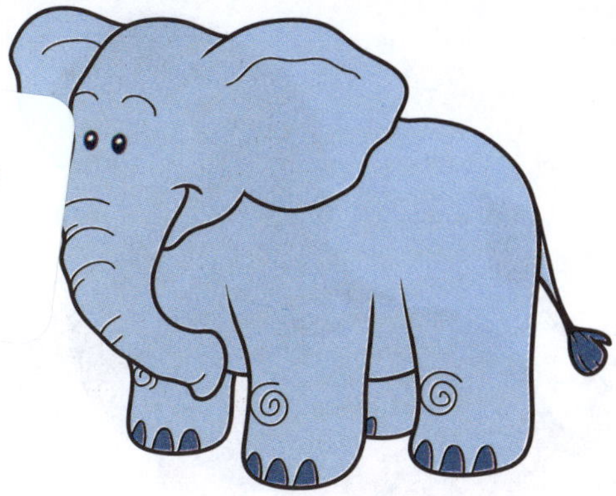

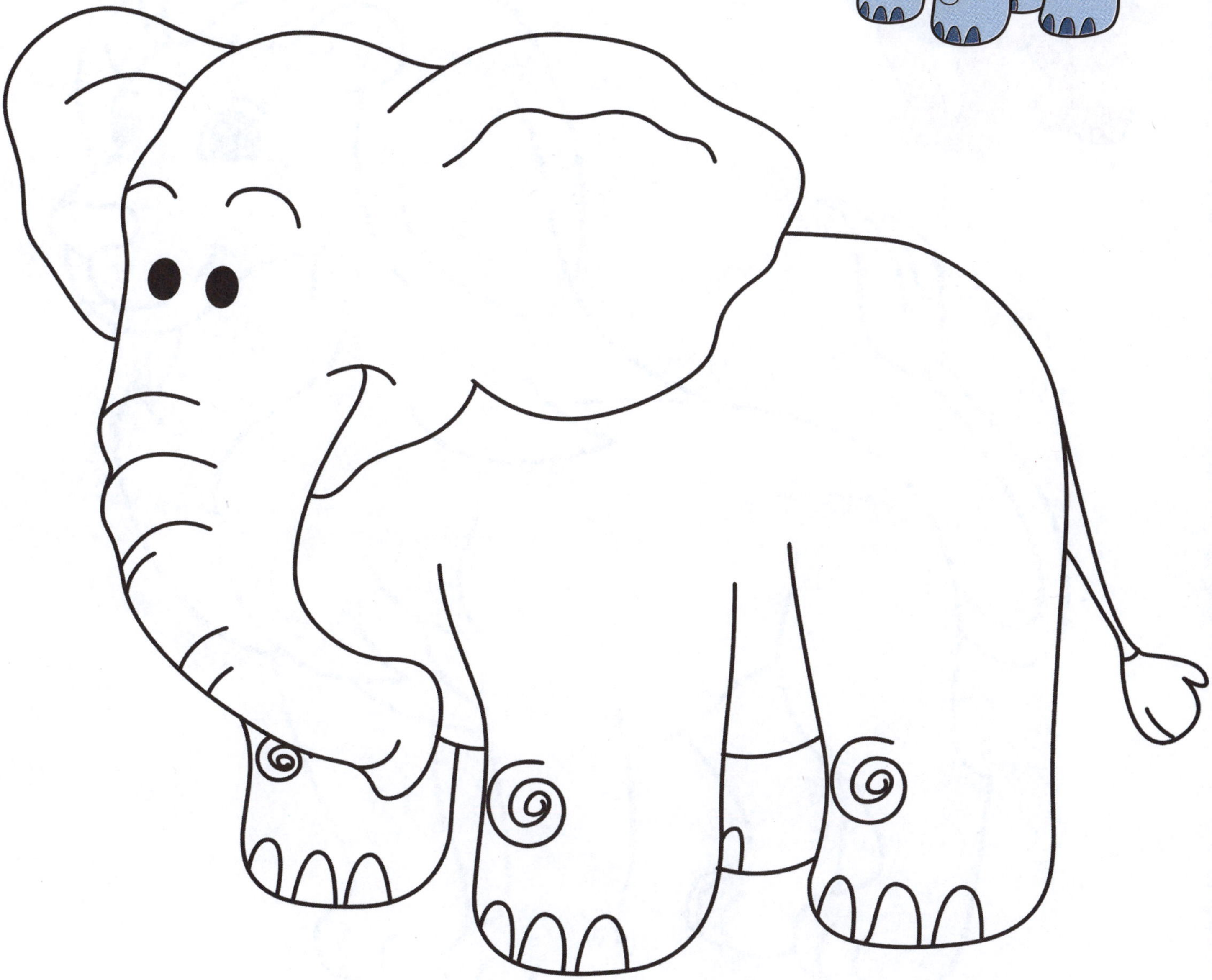

elephant

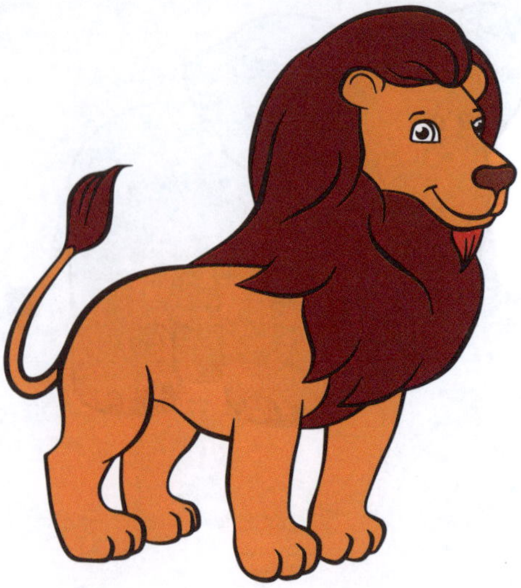

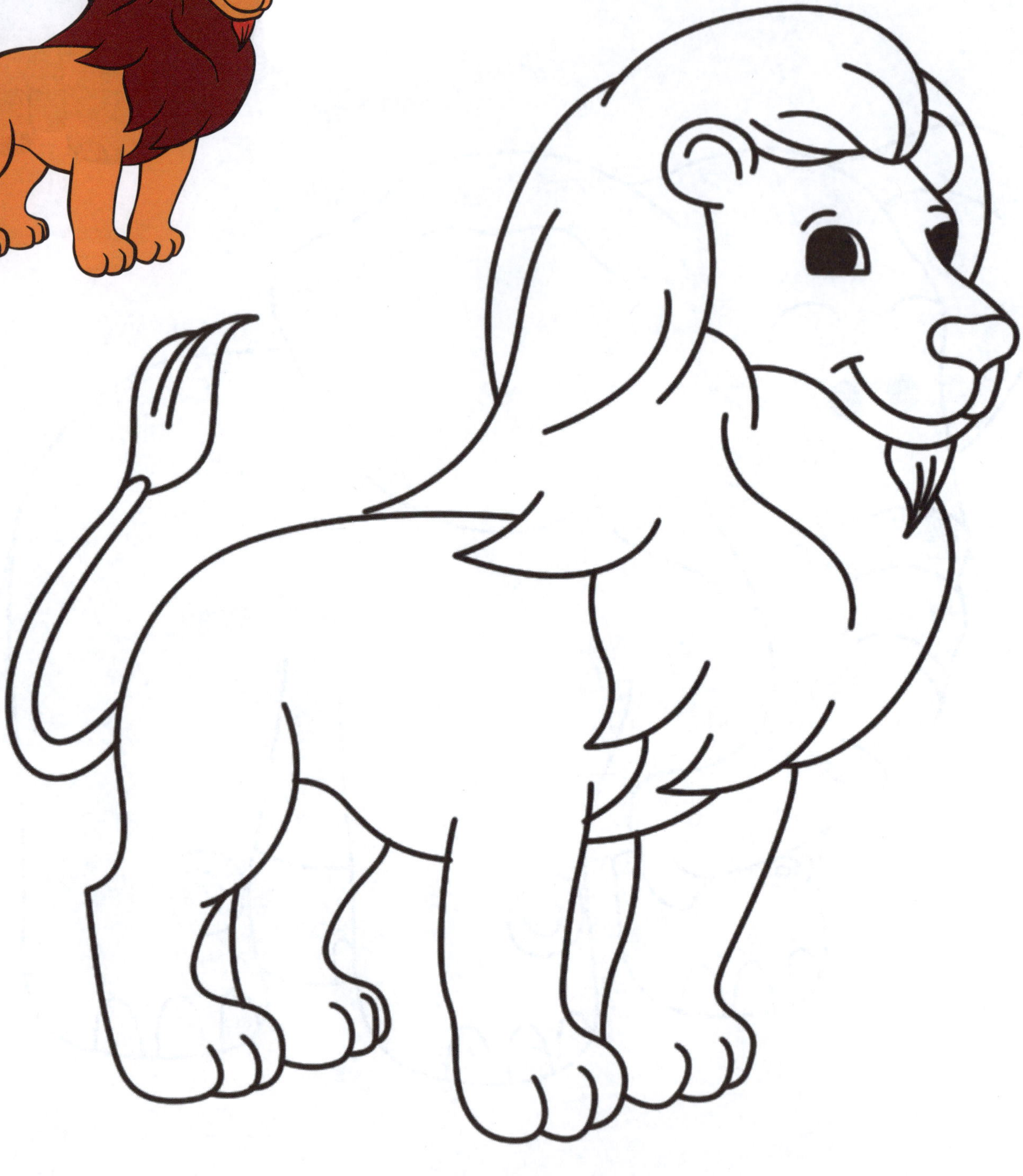

lion

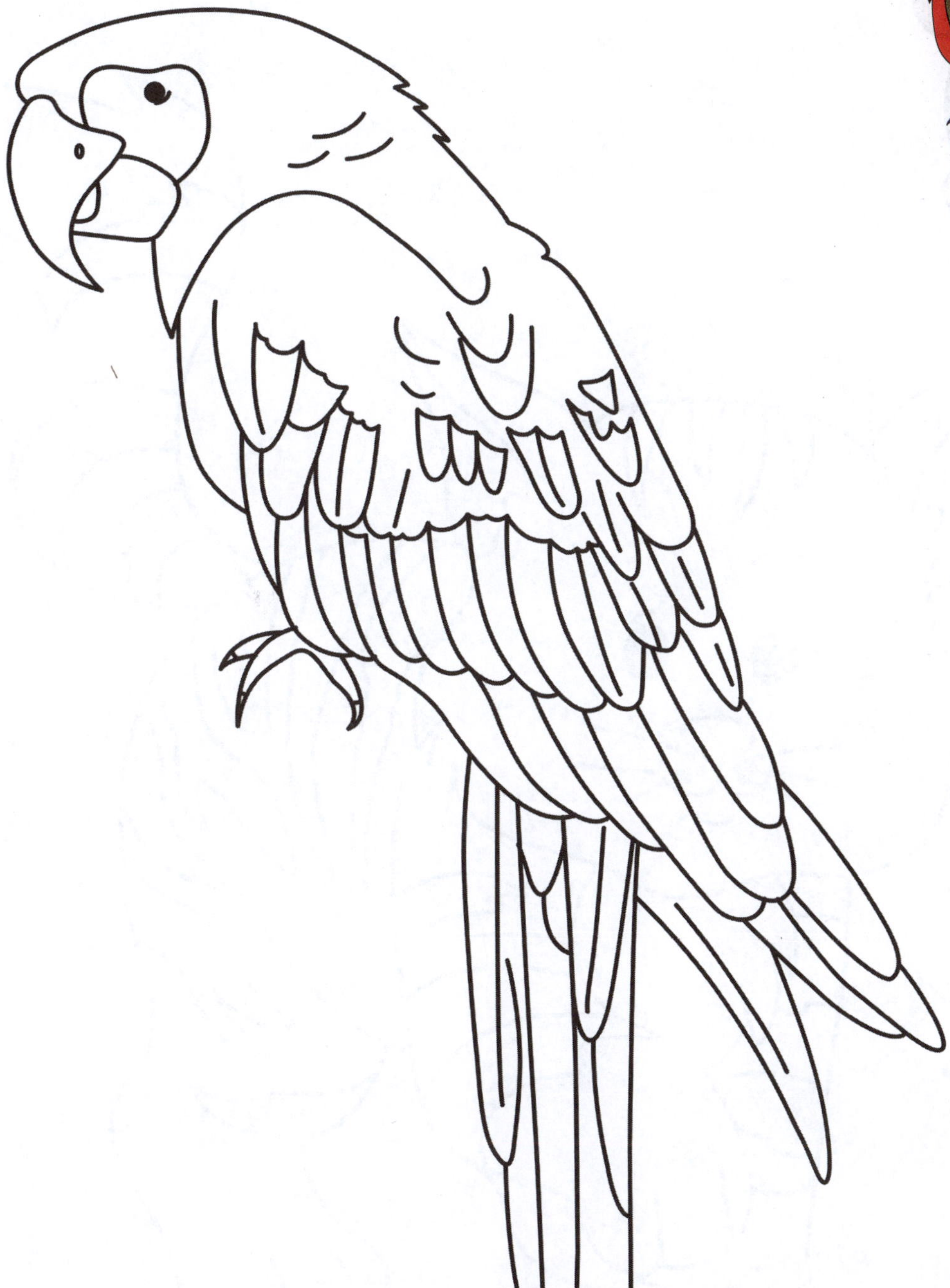

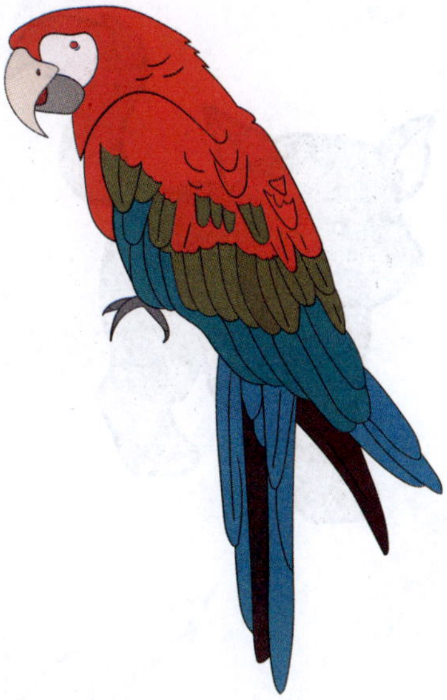

macaw

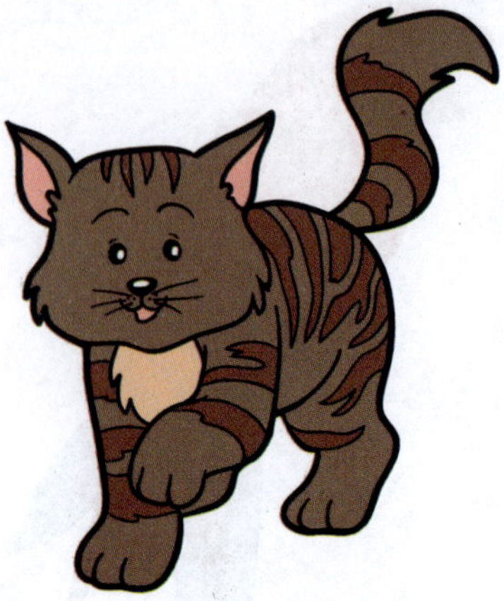

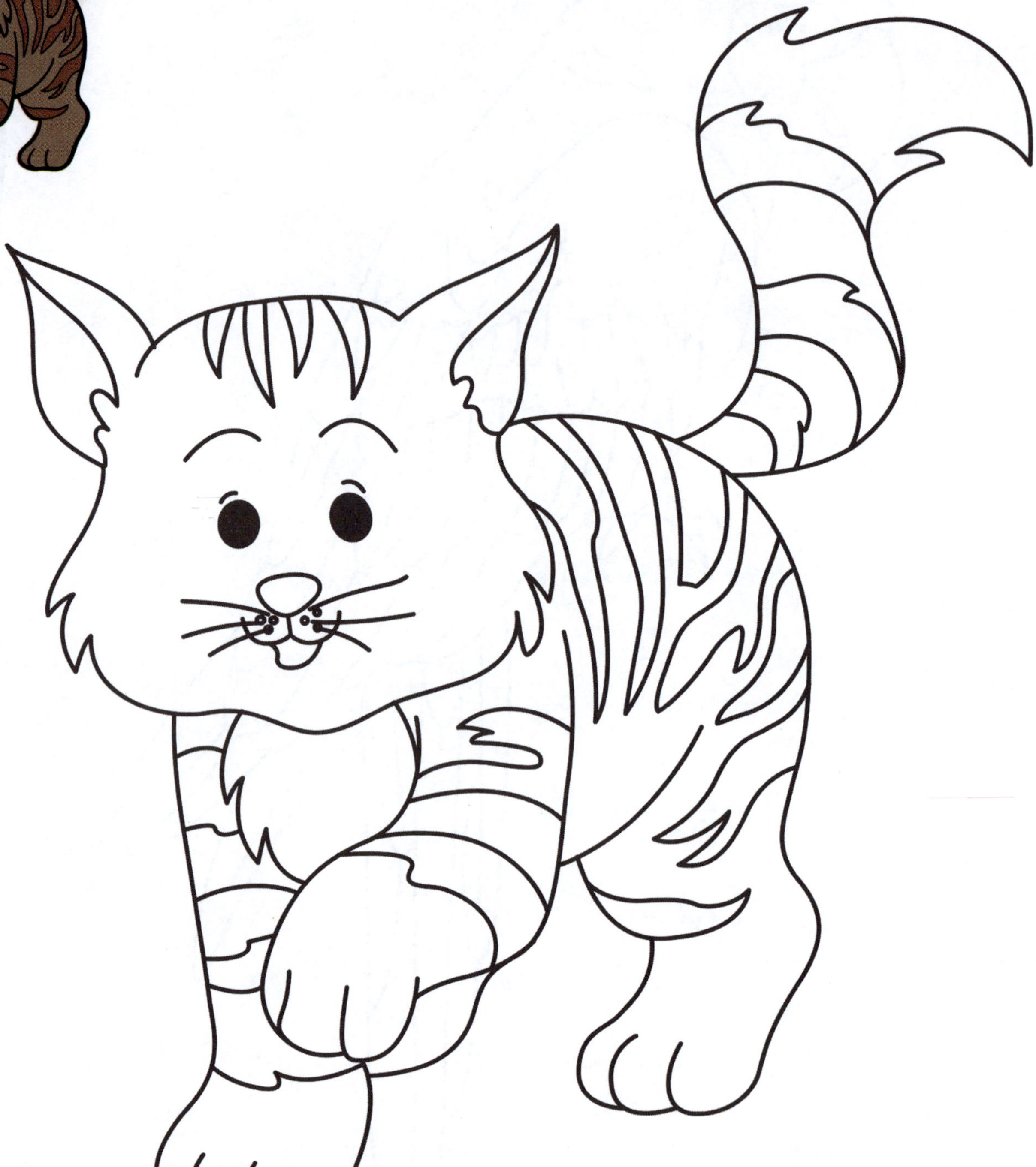

cat

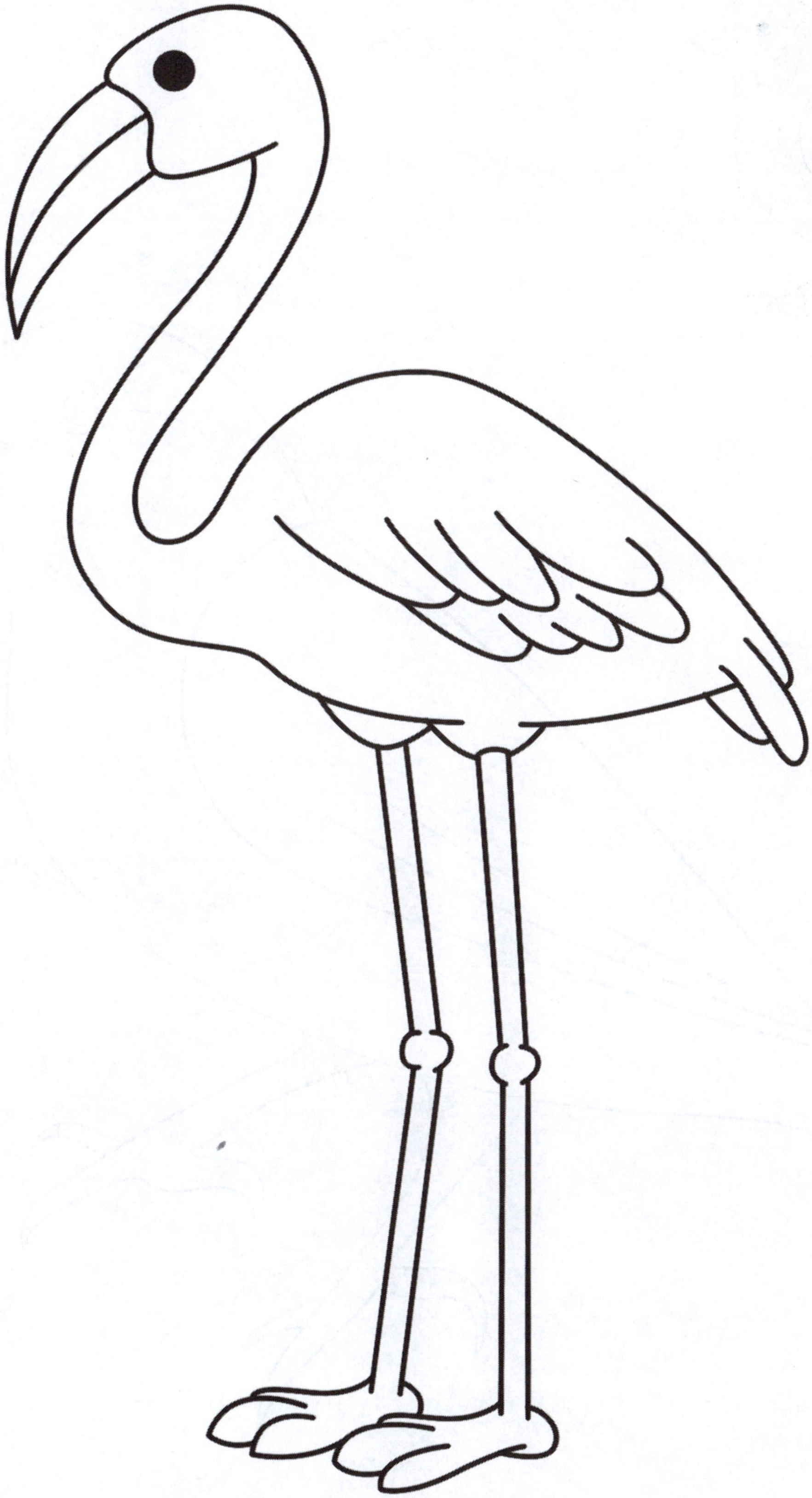

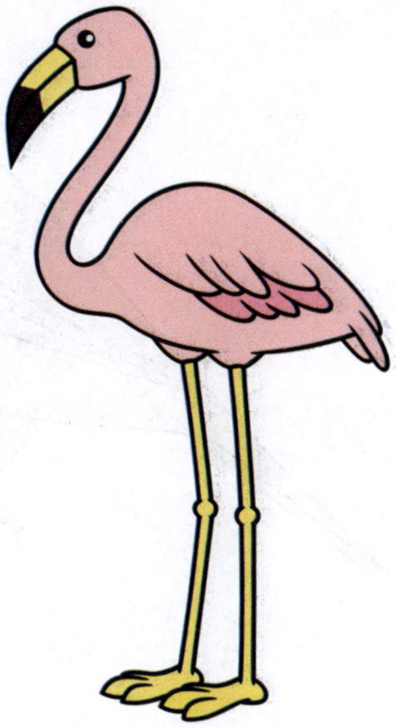

flamingo

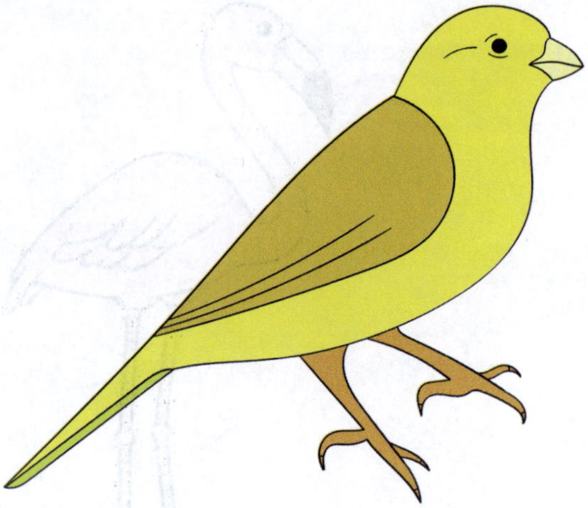

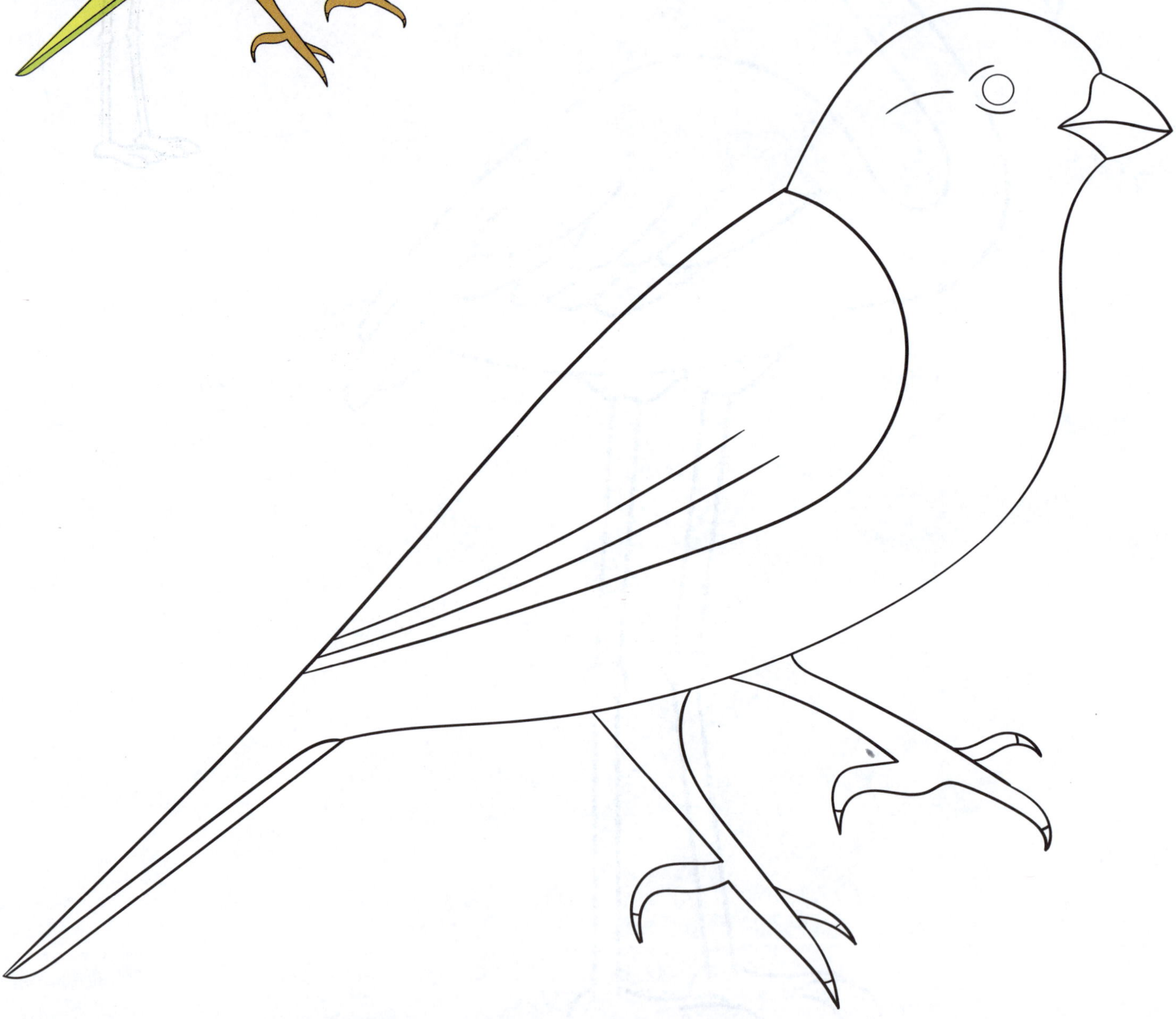

canary

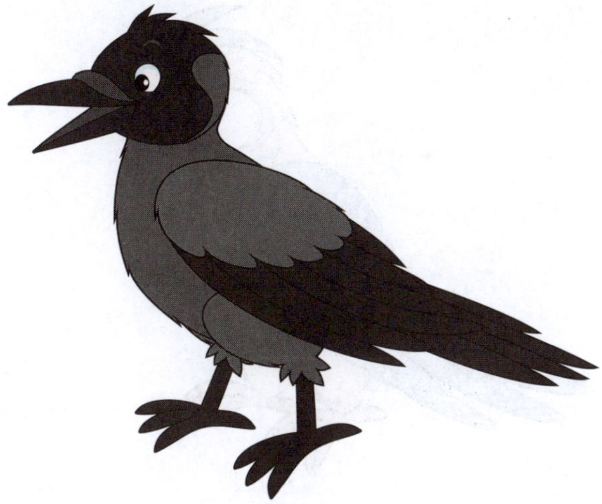

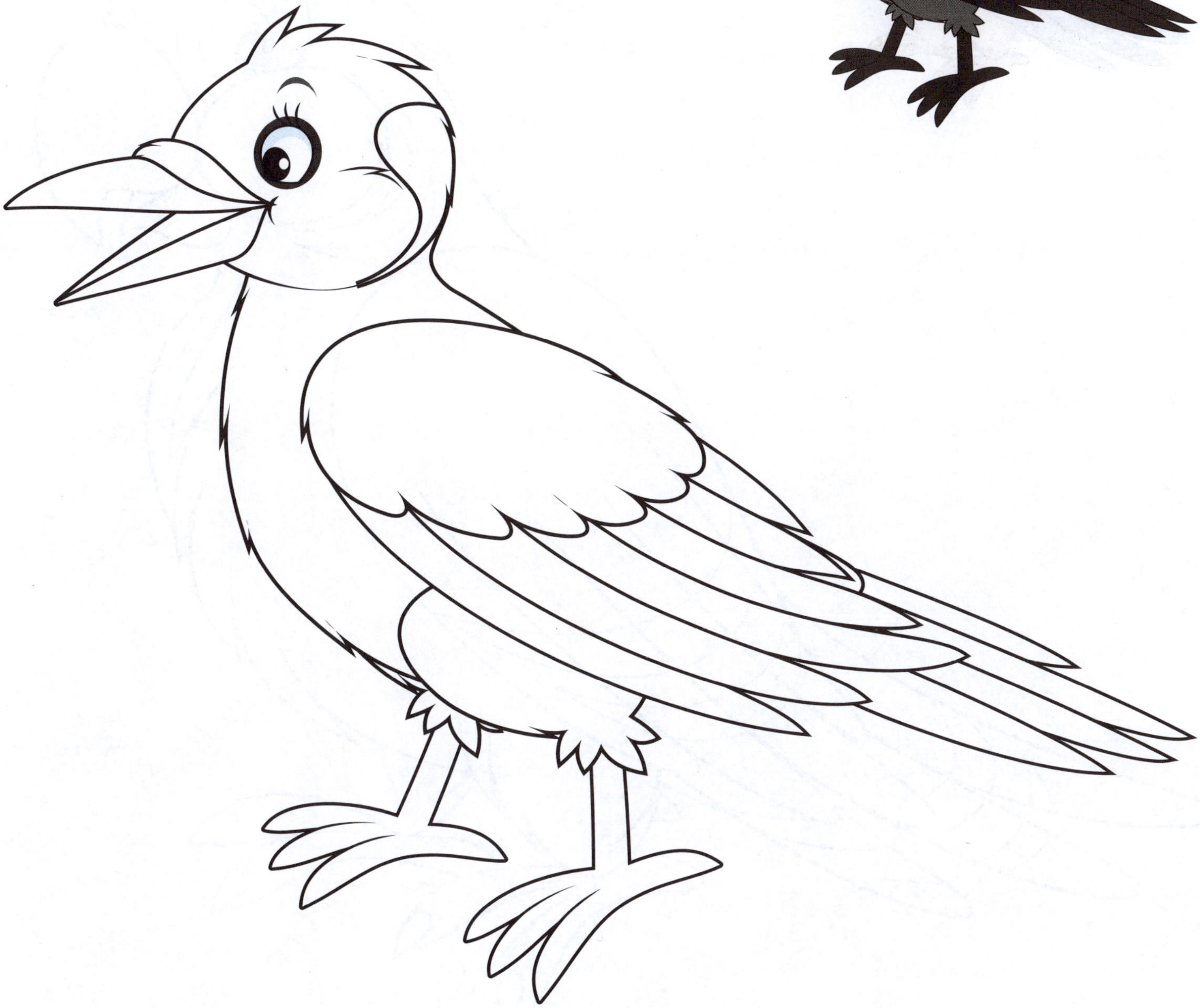

crow

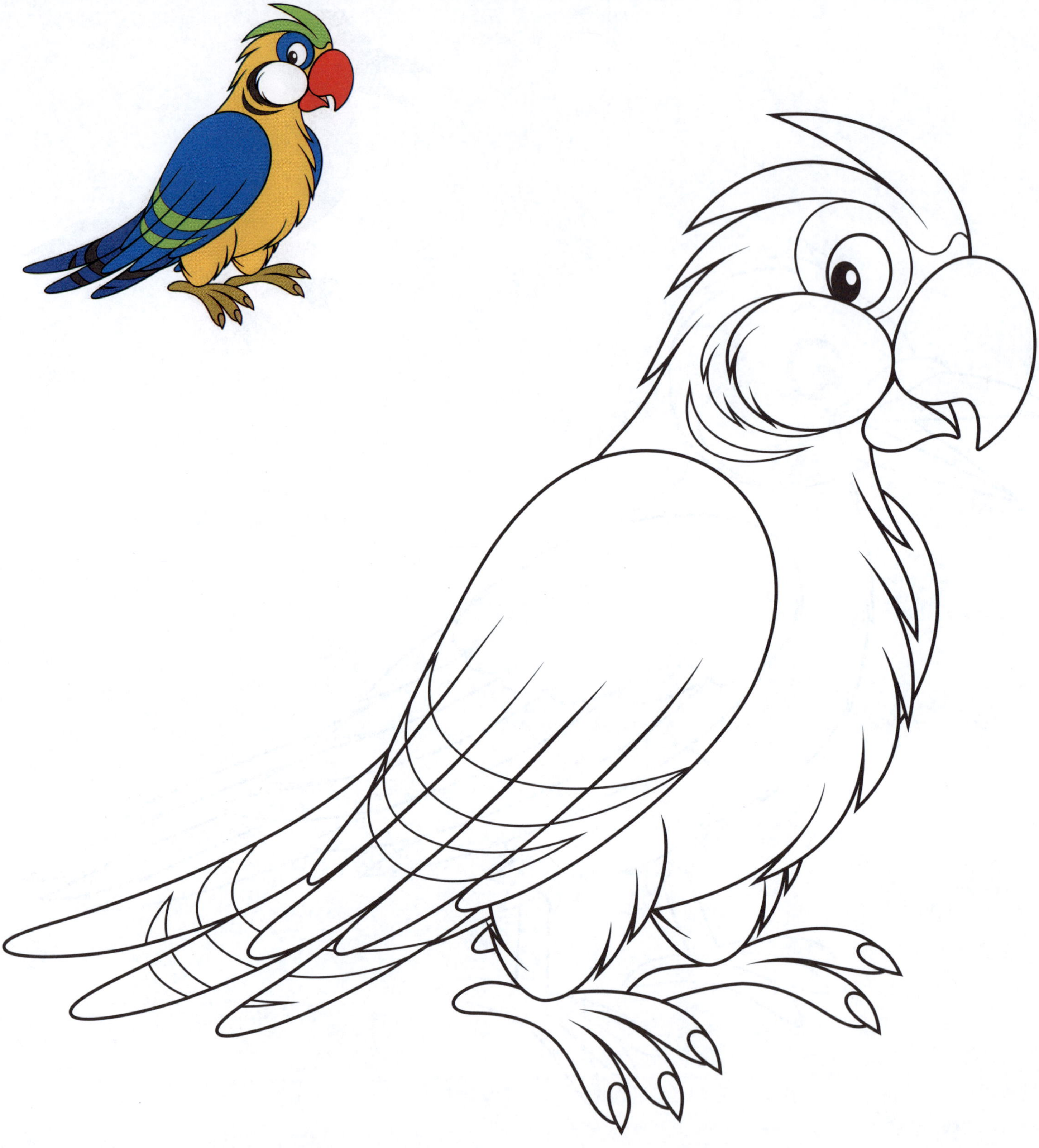

parrot

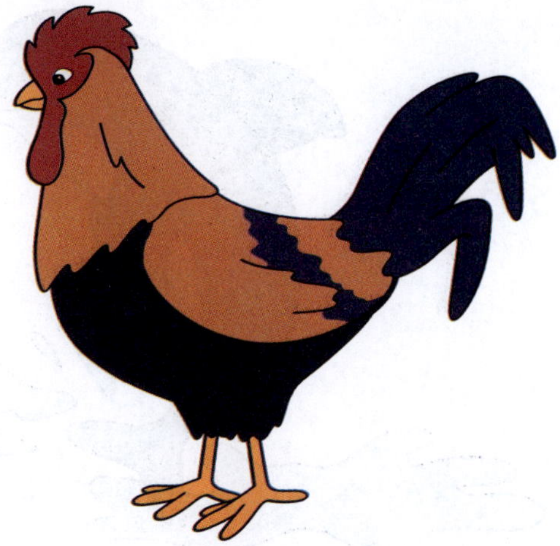

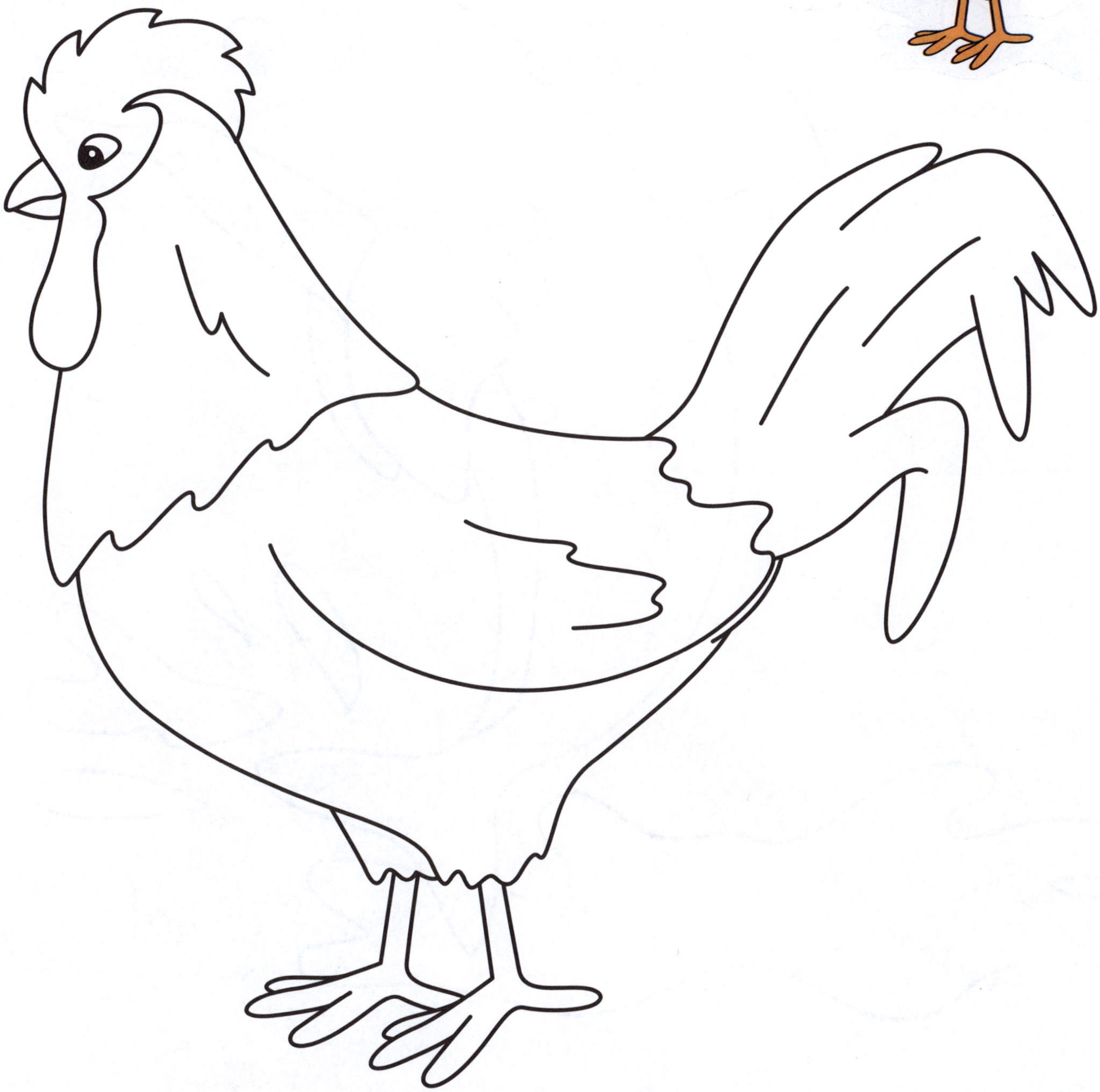

rooster

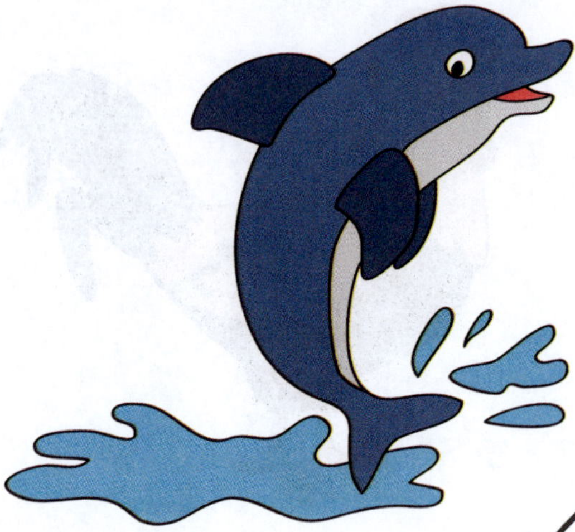

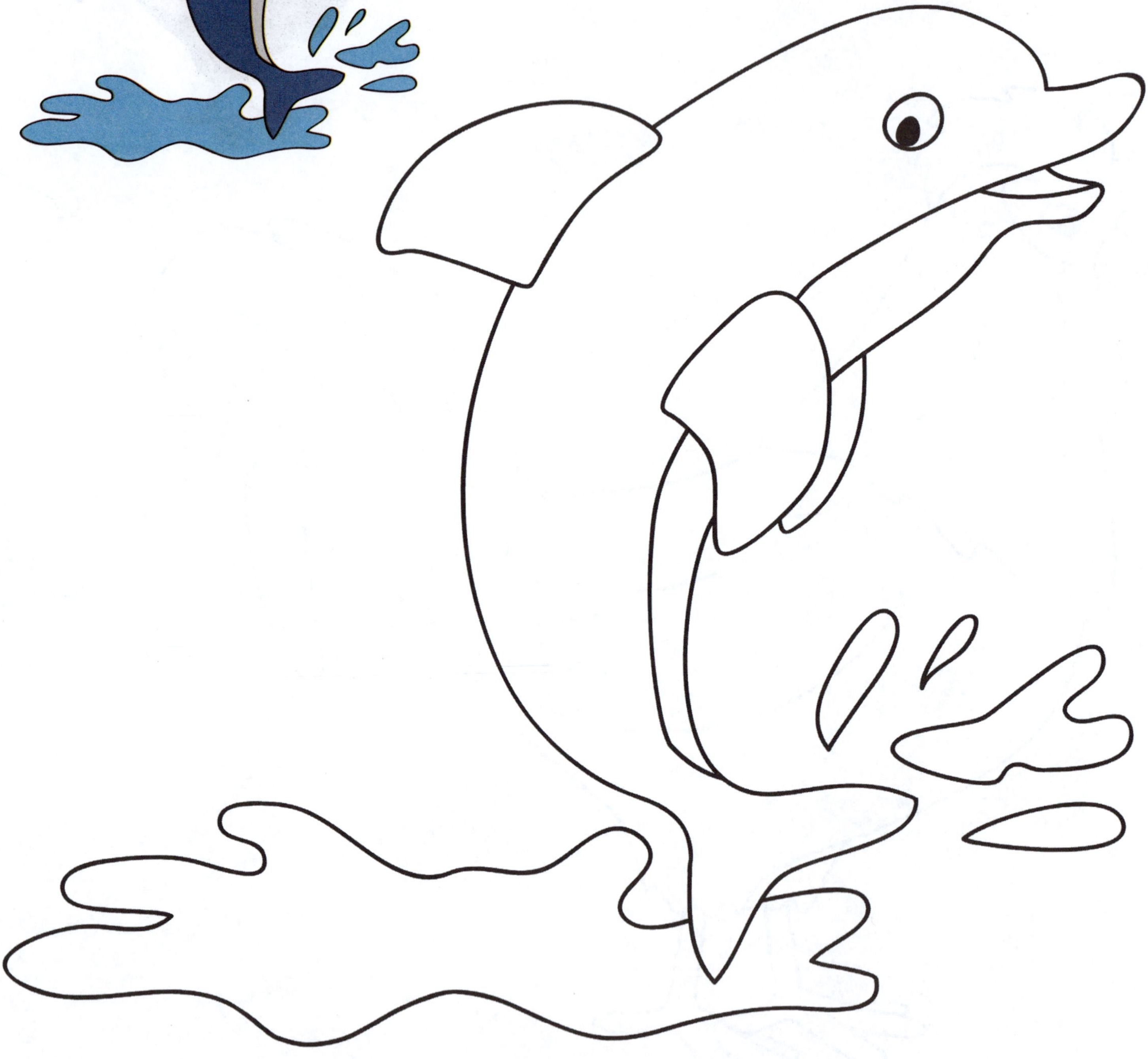

dolphin

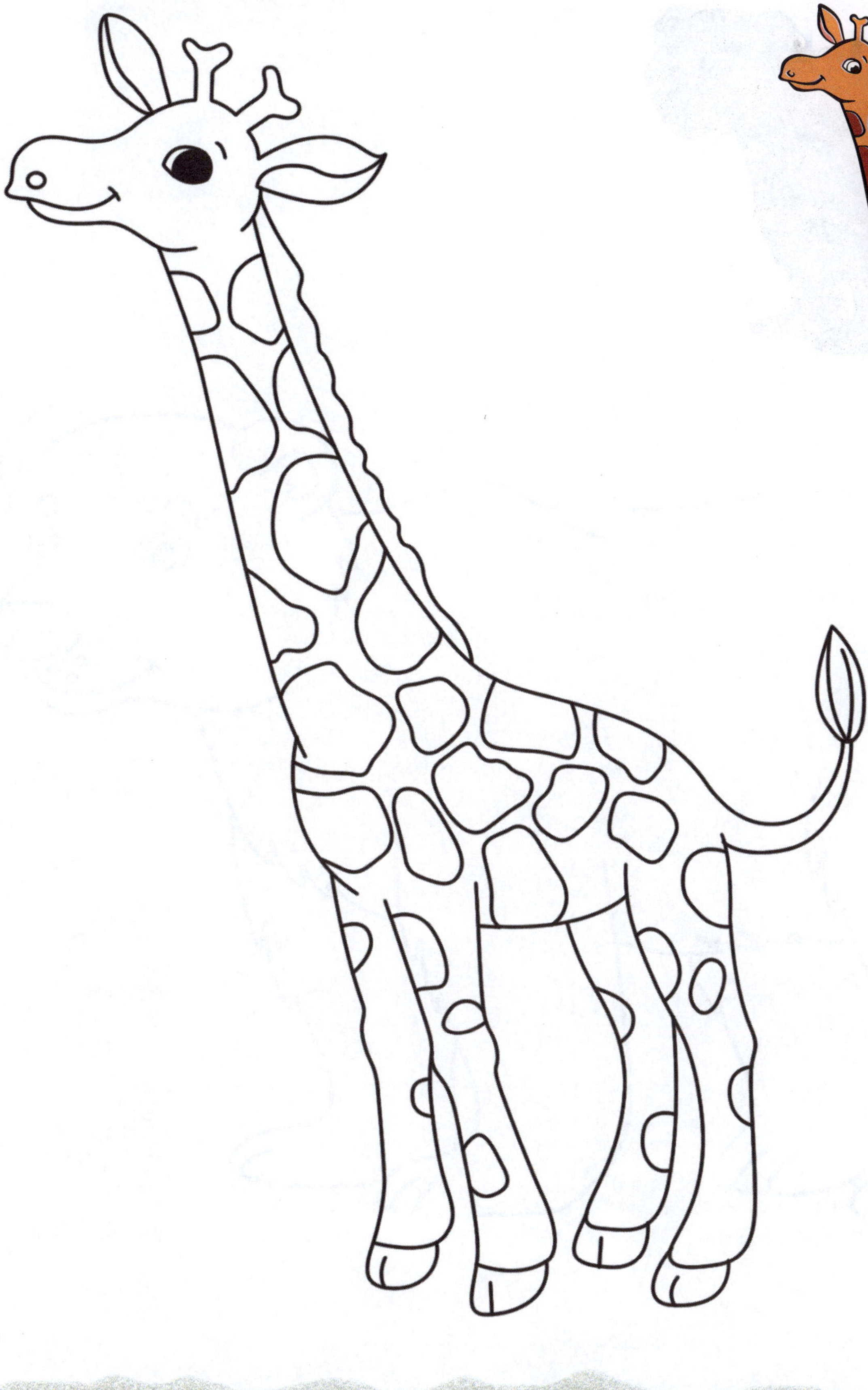

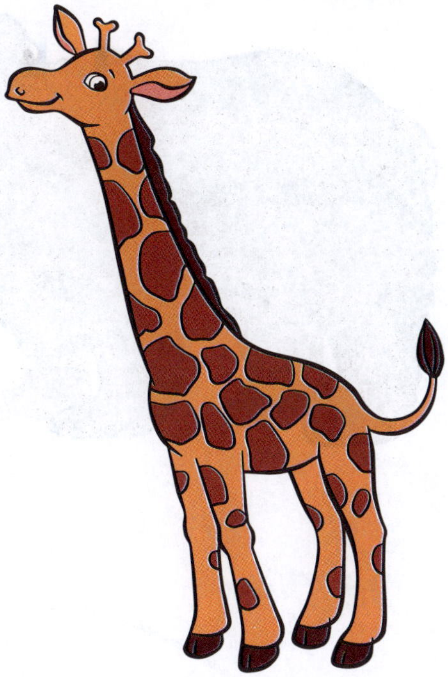

giraffe

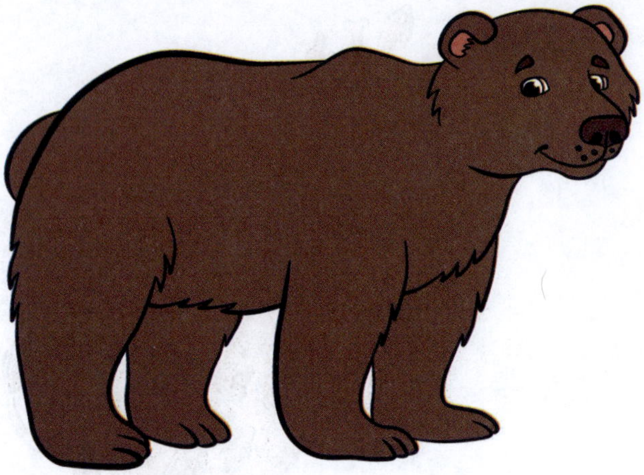

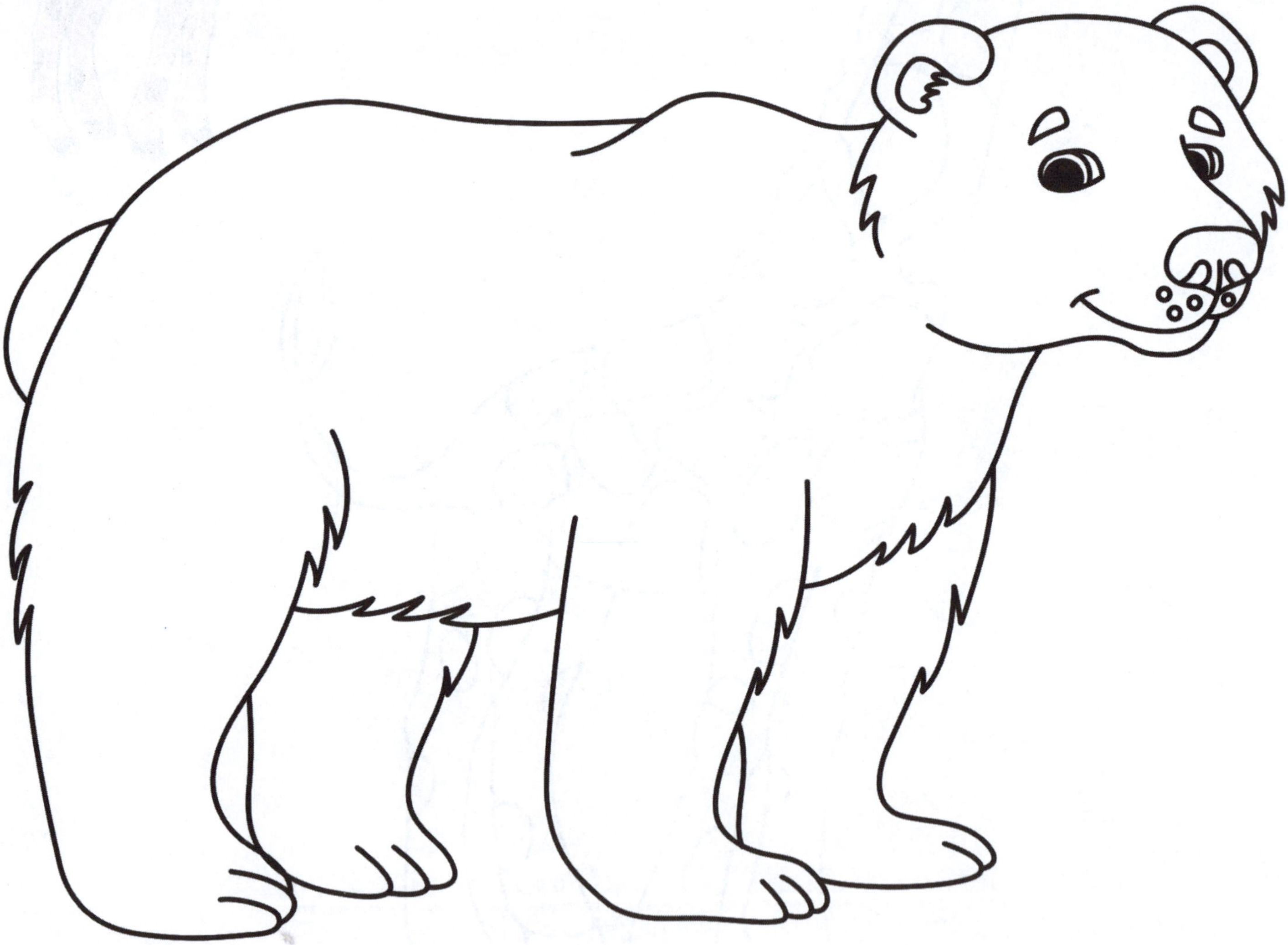

bear

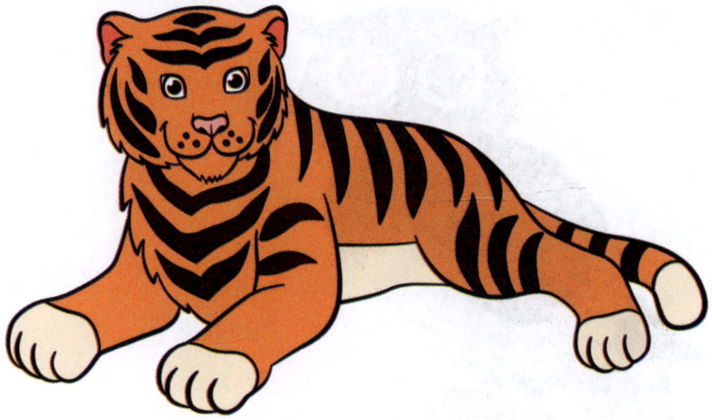

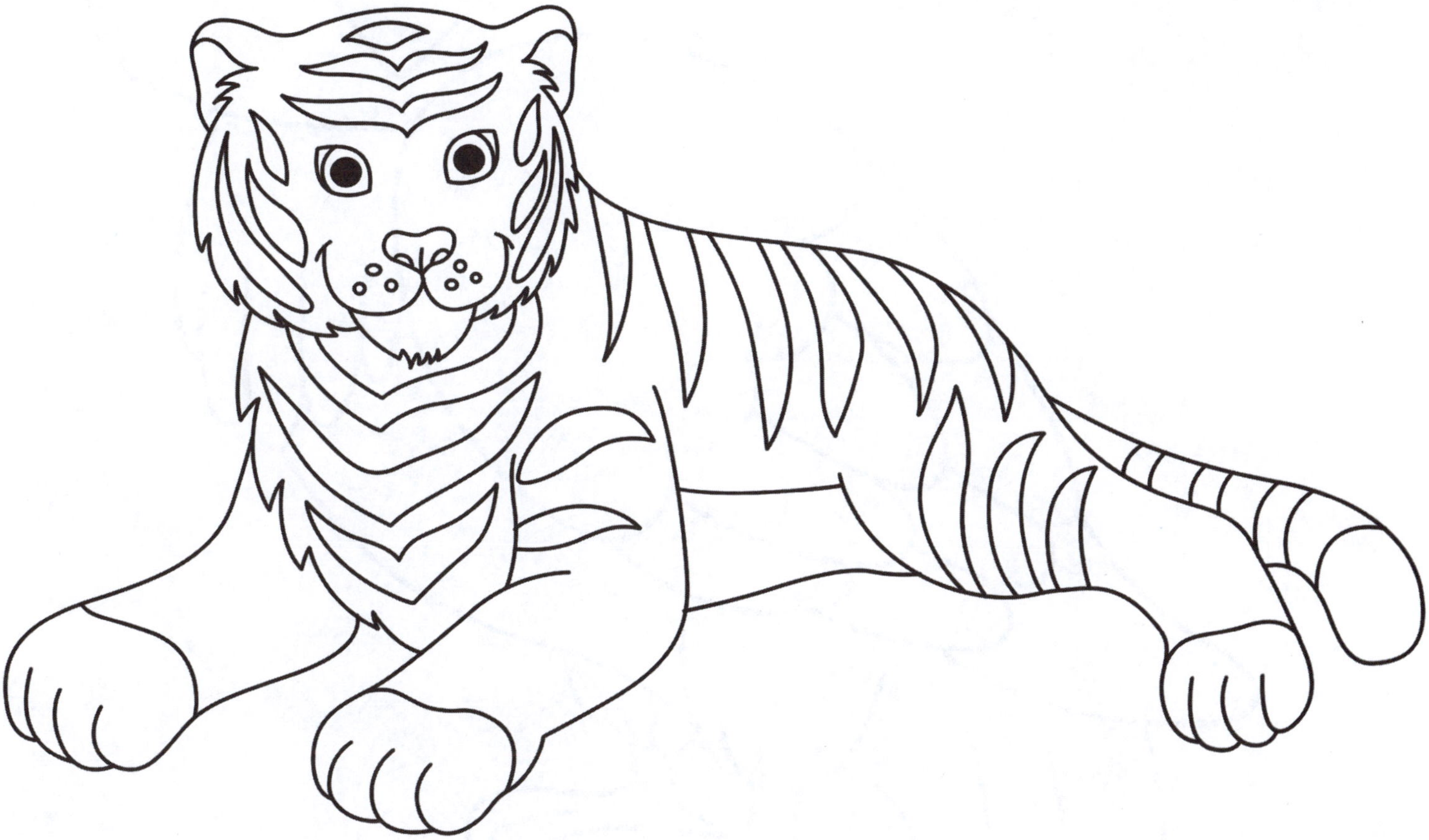

tiger

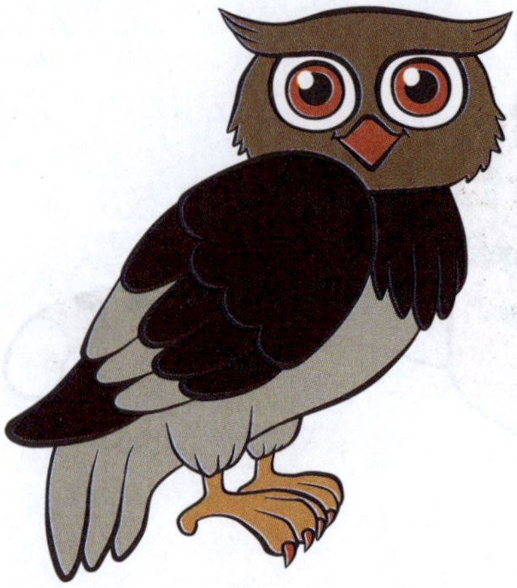

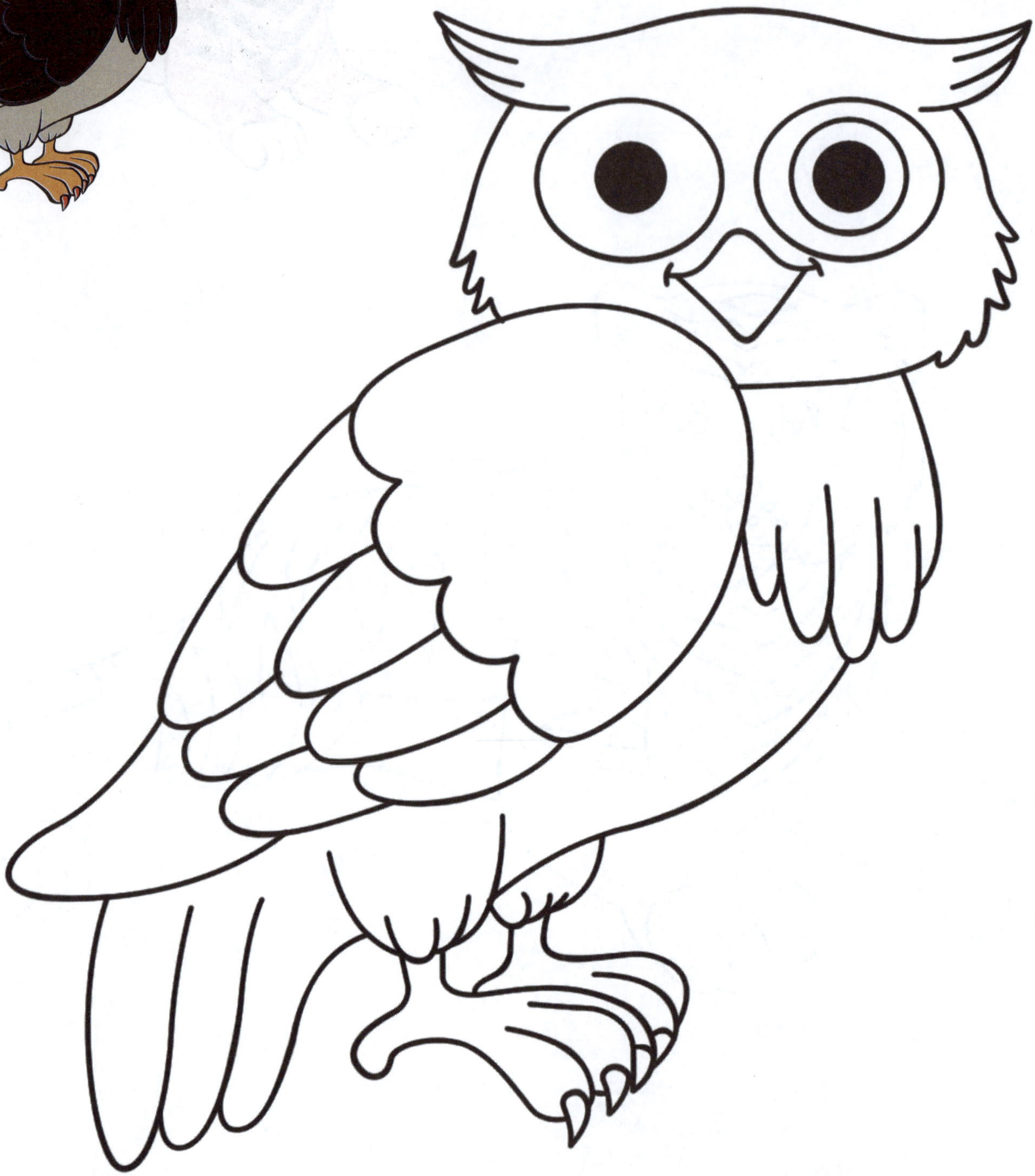

owl

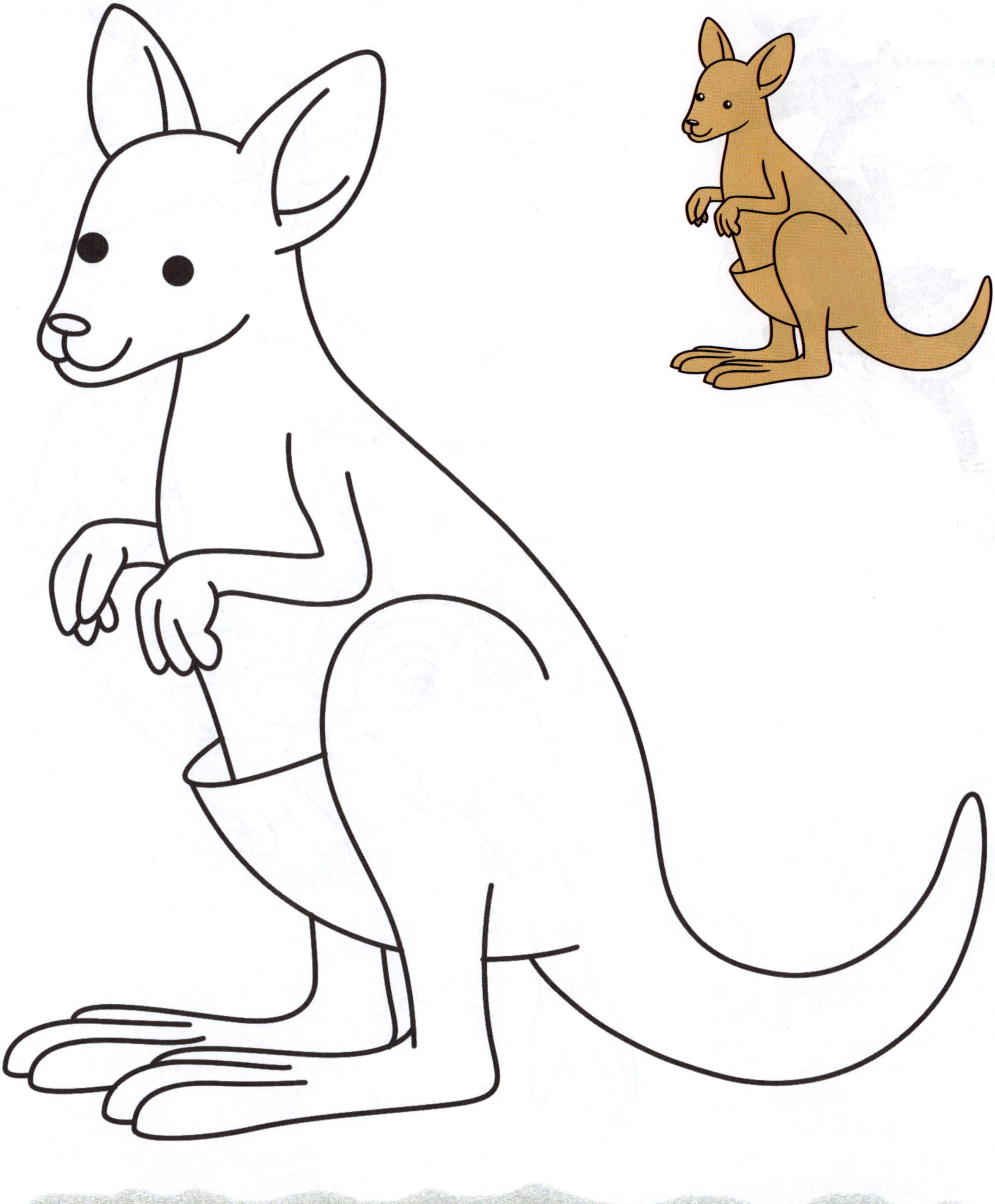

kangaroo

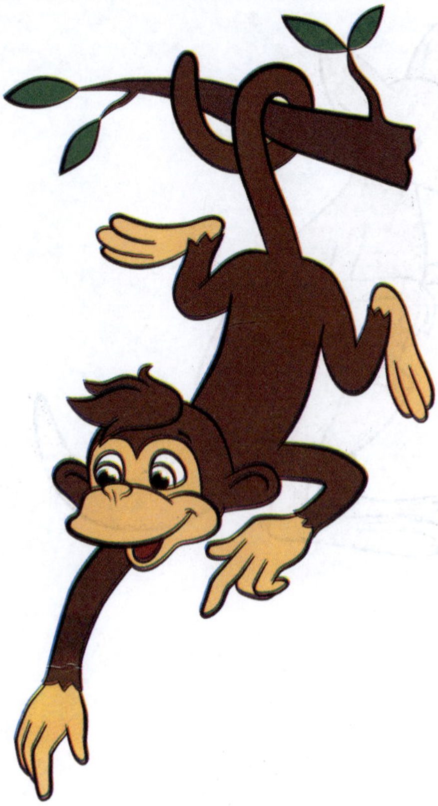

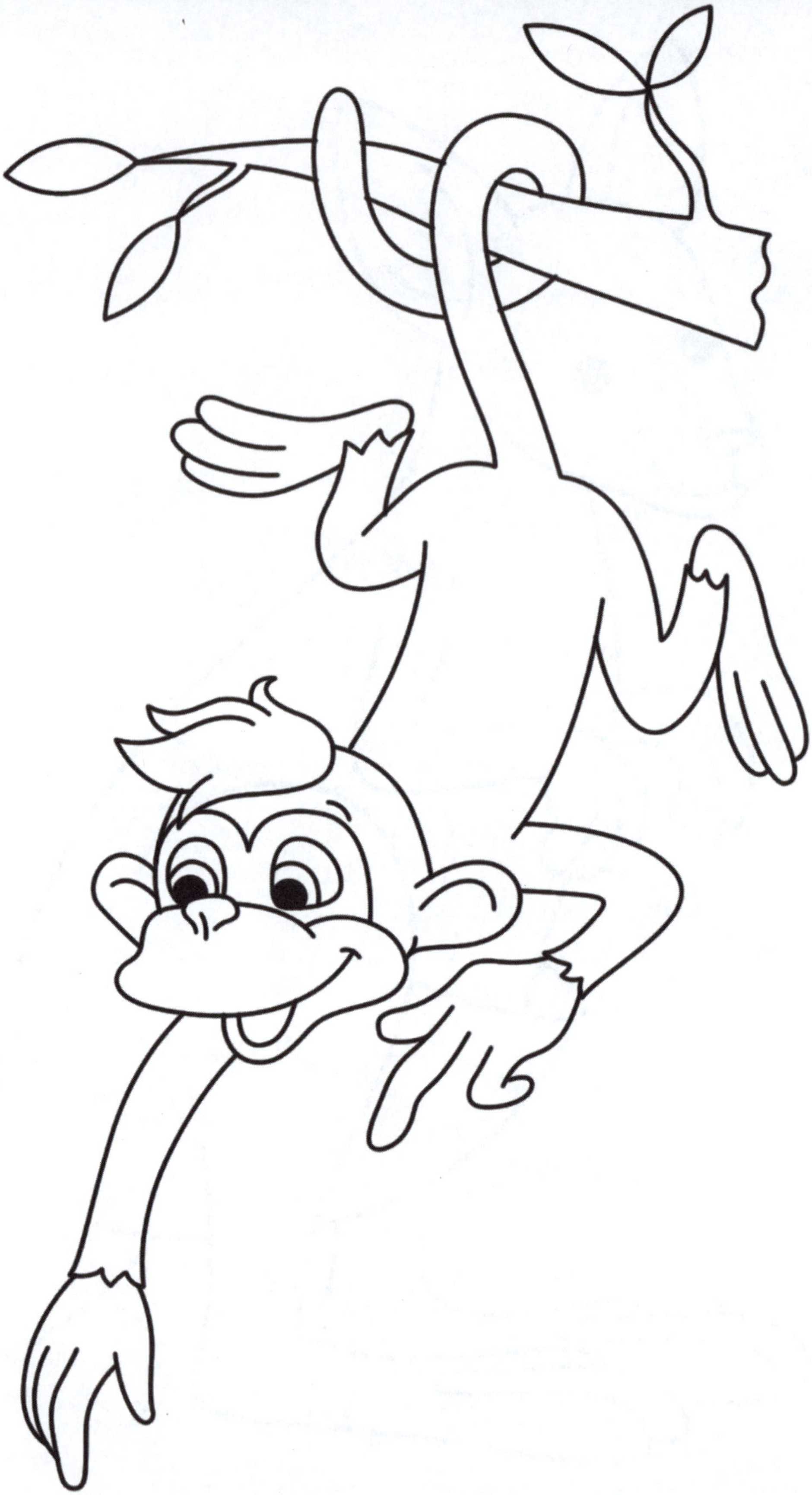

monkey